MW00948709

The Appalachian Trail, Step by Step

How to Prepare for a Thru or Long Distance Section Hike.

By

Tommy "Freerange" Bailey

Cover Art by Missy Blake

1st Edition Copyright 2012
2nd Edition Copyright 2014

Free Range Press
Willis, VA 24380
www.treestonevillage.com

All rights reserved. This book may only be referenced if proper citation is given to the author and publisher. In other words, give me a little credit and you can use what you want.

Contents

Introduction...5

State of Mind 8

Section hiking Vs. Thru-hiking.................................10

Brief History of the Appalachian Trail....................13

Attitude 15

Weight..19

Gear...22

Backpack 24

Footwear...27

Socks and Liners..30

Sleeping Bags 34

Sleeping Mats...36

Clothes 38

Cook Stove 40

Cook Set 42

Shelter...44

Water Filters & Containers 47

Trekking Poles 51

Rain Gear..53

Lighting...55

AT Literature & Maps...56

First Aid Kit...59

Stuff Sacks..60

Toiletries 61

Mobile Phones 62

Miscellaneous 63

On the AT 64

How many miles a day should I hike?.....................65

Water 69

Shelters 72

Mail Drops vs. Town Resupply 74

Towns..78

Other Hikers...81

Pets 85

Wildlife...87

Views & Scenery 90

Leave No Trace...92

Food 94

To Cook or Not to Cook...95

What Kind of Food and How Much..96
Breakfast 97
Lunch..98
Dinner 99
Desserts & Snacks 103
You Be the Judge...105
How Many Days of Food to Carry 106
Typical Rations for a 6-Day Hike 109
Ending Your Hike...110
Attitude Revisited 111
Physical Limitations...112
Financial Woes..114
Completion 116
Give of Yourself..117
Appendix...118
Trial Run 119
Trail Magic..120
Organizations of Interest 122
Gear Checklist 123

Introduction

Welcome to the Appalachian Trail, Step by Step. What you are about to read is the product of section hiking the entire Appalachian Trail (AT) over the course of fourteen years. This book is primarily a *how-to* book on preparing for a long distance or thru hike of the AT; covering all aspects of gear, food, logistics, and mental attitude needed to prepare for a successful hike. You will find plenty of anecdotes woven into the pages to put things in perspective and explain why I have come to certain conclusions about gear, food, footwear, et cetera.

This book is primarily for beginning hikers, but also serves to expand the knowledge necessary for day and weekend backpackers to successfully plan and hike the AT.

Most of my section hikes on the AT have been solo, but early on I completed several sections with partners. I mention my brother and former hiking partner, Paul, a lot because we started the trail together down at Springer Mountain, Georgia. A few years and several hundred miles later, Amber joined me to hike from southern Virginia to southern Pennsylvania.

Paul's companionship, constructive criticism and different perspectives on hiking made the early days of our section hikes very rich and rewarding. Amber's companionship on the trail brought on a new sense of enjoying the wilderness with someone I love and admire very much. Her spirit of adventure and strong determination during our 600+ miles on the trail will always be remembered and cherished.

I've read this manuscript many times and am constantly revising parts of it – taking out and even rewriting whole paragraphs and pages. In short, even now this is a work in progress. I am beginning to believe nothing in life can ever be 'finished'. That's what's so special about our existence; we are always learning and growing as long as we wish to. When we cease to learn or grow and just accept our lives as static, can we really hope to be wholly satisfied with this game of life we are playing? I don't know the answer to that yet, but I do know I am offering you a piece of what I have experienced on the Appalachian Trail. I hope it will benefit or enrich your life in some way; not only on preparing for and hiking the trail, but in everyday situations.

I hope by offering this how-to on the AT, you will have the opportunity to get on the trail and experience the awesome life-changing events that can happen out there. Use the AT as a catalyst to enrich your life – as it will most certainly do.

Whether you are a beginner or weekend warrior, this book will guide you step-by-step, through all you will need to know to get started. Hiking the Appalachian Trail is definitely a test of the body, mind and spirit. May you have the will to stay strong on your journey and the courage to finish your thru or individual section hikes. Congratulations on considering the AT challenge and may your hike be a grand one. See you on the trail!

I have been told there are three reasons people hike the Appalachian Trail. They are:

-- Running away from something.

-- Searching for something.

-- Out for the adventure of it

In my experience and through observation of other hikers on the trail, I have to say you will probably fit into one or more of these categories.

My intentions for first hiking the Appalachian Trail were a mix of all three. I was in a place in my life where I was not particularly happy with who I was and what I was doing. Consequently, I started doing a lot of soul searching, trying to figure out what I wanted out of life. I was running full blast away from my then present life in search of something more meaningful when I decided to hike the Appalachian Trail. Gaining clarity in my life was a big motivating factor why I wanted to hike the AT, but I have to say adventure and excitement were also main driving forces that enabled me to set up such an elaborate trip.

I have always enjoyed the woods and could always find peace there. Besides looking at the Appalachian Trail as a grand adventure, I felt like it was a vision quest of sorts to revealing my inner most thoughts and desires. To find out what my next move in life should be.

Paul and I planned our first trip on the AT and it was successful. Two and a half months after we started, I came off the trail with a clear mind, ready to take on the world again. I had a whole new list of goals I wanted to pursue and I was re-energized enough to go for them. One of these goals was to let others know how special the AT is and what they might be able to gain from it. Many miles and more than a few years later, I have attempted to do just that with this book.

Section hiking Vs. Thru-hiking

In 2000 my brother Paul and I had the opportunity to start out on the Appalachian Trail. That first summer we had a combined total of $700 and all the time in the world to go as far as we possibly could. It took us two months and the whole $700 to hike four hundred and fifty-five miles. Miles were not important to us then. Who cared if we did four miles or twenty; our focus was to enjoy the experience and not rush it.

So we decided we were best cut out being section hikers, long distance ones. In retrospect I am grateful we decided to do it that way, rather than try and finish the whole trail in one or two trips. Having the trail to look forward to every year or two has been wonderful on many levels.

In our early section hikes, we developed a day-by-day attitude. We hiked according to what our bodies and minds dictated and, of course, by how much food we could carry. On that first trip we averaged just over seven miles a day. Some days we would hike twelve miles, other days we would find a nice area and not hike at all. We learned quickly that not getting in a hurry was the method for us. Seeing, experiencing and being in nature, and meeting other hikers, was so much more important to us than trying to hike X number of miles per day. Plus, it was tremendously fulfilling experiencing the trail at this pace. Just like anything in life, if you take it a little slower, the experience is always fuller and more meaningful than if you breeze through it.

Though thru-hiking is not for me, it appeals to others. Thru-hikers are definitely a different breed than most. They set a goal of reaching the end -- Katahdin for North-bounders or Springer Mountain for South-bounders -- and go for it. Not much will stop them, barring a major physical ailment, from completing their goal.

To thru-hike the whole trail in one trek you must be extremely focused and prepare to hike twenty plus miles each day. You can get there averaging fifteen miles a day, but you would be pushing it weather wise. It might very well be snowing in Maine by the time you get there and, believe it or not, the southern states can get bitter cold and produce a lot of snow in the fall.

I have heard stories of thru-hikers taking as long as eleven months (they left and came back in the same year) to only three months to hike the entire Appalachian Trail. It all boils down to the amount of miles you want to hike and what you want from the experience.

I truly admire the determination and stamina of a thru-hiker. It is an awesome challenge. To complete this long hike in one trek says a whole lot about the mentality and physical condition of the person doing it. Now that I've finished section hiking the trail, who knows, maybe I'll be inspired to thru-hike it next time!

I wish I could give you a little more insight about thru-hiking, but I can only write what I know and I know long distance section hiking well. Again, regardless whether you want to thru or section hike the

AT, the following pages will help you prepare either way. But before we move on, I must provide a brief history of the Appalachian Trail for you.

Brief History of the Appalachian Trail

The Appalachian Trail was the brainchild of a man named Benton Makaye. He had envisioned a great trail running north to south from New England to the southern Appalachian Mountains. In 1921, heeding the advice of his friends and colleagues, Makaye published his *Project in Regional Planning* in the Journal of American Institute of Architects.

In 1923 some of the first miles of trail were already developed and designed specifically as the Appalachian Trail. By 1925 the Appalachian Trail Conference (ATC) was officially founded in Washington D.C. The ATC works closely with the National Park Service to maintain and protect the 2100 plus miles of the Appalachian Trail. Finally, in 1968 Congress passed the National Trail Systems Act ensuring the protection of the Appalachian Trail under the federal government.

The rest is history…evolving! The ATC, now renamed the Appalachian Trail Conservancy, has relocated to Harpers Ferry, WV, and has a lead role in protecting and maintaining the Appalachian Trail along with numerous volunteer hiking and trail clubs. Today, less than one percent of the Appalachian Trail is located along private lands. The ATC vigorously continues to acquire and protect the remaining private land near the trail. I am positive we wouldn't have the Appalachian Trail as we know it today without the ATC. May they keep up their wonderful efforts in managing and maintaining the AT and gain more support in conservation efforts as encroachments and developing of natural areas becomes more widespread.

Attitude

Attitude is key on the trail. If you don't have a positive and open attitude you are guaranteed to have a miserable hike, especially on days when your body aches and you are soaked from head to toe. You might have some bad days out there, but don't let them get you down because the Appalachian Trail is a beautiful experience if you let it be.

My attitude on the trail is to take it day-by-day, enjoying everything the trail has to offer, even the rain. People complain about the rain, but I know it is easy to forget that the trees desperately need the water and, in turn, do not the mountain streams flow down to fill our reservoirs, rivers and other water supplies? No one wants to get soaked when they are out hiking, but it is possible to change your mind about it. You can accept the rain and enjoy the day, or you can complain about the rain and probably have a miserable day. It's all in our control to have a good time or a bad one. Remember this because you will have days on the trail in which you will have to remind yourself!

If Paul or Amber or I did not lose sight of our day-by-day attitude, by making negative assumptions and building mounds of expectations, the trail always produced awesome experiences for us. Whether it was realizing the simple beauty of nature, encountering trail magic, or having pleasurable encounters with other hikers, we always felt like we were in the *flow*.

Another way to keep an attitude in check is to take *Zero's* – that is, to take a day off and not hike at all. Taking time to rest along the trail was very important to my mental and physical wellbeing. If I found myself getting negative, discouraged or just plain beat down, a day off with my feet propped was the best medicine to cure my problems. Usually, the next day I was motivated to get back on the trail and did so with enthusiasm and vigor.

As a section hiker I was never really out long enough to deeply experience some of the problems thru-hikers faced after being on the trail for months at a time. Here is a prime example of the mindset it takes to be a thru-hiker, even early on. I met a thru-hiker in Tennessee on his way to Maine. We were resting at a shelter eating a snack when I saw a hiker take off his boots to tend his feet. I looked over and noticed one of his feet looked like one gigantic blister. It was bad, the worst I have ever seen. He even cut out the side of his boot because one of the blisters was rubbing so badly.

He took a knife to his boot! I guess mud and water getting in his boot was second to the pain that he was feeling from the friction. This thru-hiker was going to Maine no matter what. I'm not judging this to be good or bad, it was just the attitude he needed to complete his goal of getting to Maine. Not all thru-hikers are that hard-core but they do have a goal in mind and set out to accomplish it. Just be safety minded and don't overdo it.

I have come to the conclusion that hiking the AT (or anything in life) is mostly mental and less physical.

The body is capable of a lot if the mind is in control. I do know that mental attitude can make or break your hike. If you've got the right attitude, your body will adjust to any situation it is put into.

If you are undisciplined or have a weak mind, the trail might prove to be a failure for you. You will be miserable and struggle the entire distance before you decide to quit. But, if you can condition (or even transcend) the mind and keep trucking, you will make leaps and bounds in your ability. Not only to hike, but also produce favorable outcomes in other areas of your life. Meeting challenges and reaching goals can do a lot for self-worth!

When it comes to the AT all it takes is shifting your focus from I can't go on to, YES, I can make it up that mountain. It is awesome to find that place, those moments when you can accomplish anything. And it serves well in the memory banks of your soul, because the next time you encounter a tough situation in life you will remember how you pulled through and do it again. So be careful in distinguishing what your physical and mental drives are on the trail. Balance is the key.

I have shared my day-by-day philosophy of hiking with thru-hikers and, even though they approach the trail differently, they agree I have a great way of hiking the AT. In the end it all boils down to what you want out of the experience. Whether you lollygag like me or breeze through it like others, it is entirely up to you. Just remember to keep your attitude and thoughts in check and make the most out of each moment you have on the precious AT.

Weight

Weight can be a crucial factor in determining how enjoyable a hike you are going to have. Also, this factor will encompass some of the most important decisions concerning your comfort and wellbeing on the trail.

When Paul and I began our first trip on the AT, we had back-breaking backpacks. Out of necessity (physical & mental health) we started unloading all the least important gear. I say least important because when we started out we thought it was all important and necessary, but we soon found out you can live on a lot less. Bare bones basics are all you should take on the trail if you want to do your back, shoulders, knees and feet a favor.

I am embarrassed to say what we sent home in those first weeks. Little did we know how green we were; after all, we were experienced weekend *campers* and didn't think twice about toting all that crap around on day and weekend hikes, but the AT quickly taught us differently! Notice the keyword *campers*. We were used to hiking nominal miles to camp out for a night or weekend and it didn't matter if we were carrying fifty pounds or more. But long distance backpacking is much different, as all of us learn when we are out there doing it. I am grateful we learned this lesson and reanalyzed our ways or else we would have never made it as far as we did that first trip.

Reducing weight can become an obsession. Hikers are constantly trying to streamline gear to reduce weight. I have seen ends of toothbrushes cut off, people removing hanging straps or other unnecessary paraphernalia from their packs and some hikers don't even carry sleeping bags or tents. I even helped Paul cut off all the sleeves and midriffs from his shirts to reduce weight!

Many folks have watched or heard Paul, Amber and I preparing for a hike and you could tell they didn't fathom the weight issue. I try to stress to them you have to hike it to understand. For instance, unless you are a very experienced backpacker, what you decide to take on the trail while in the comfort of your home will not be the case once you start hiking. After a few miles of toting the heavy stuff you will quickly regret it and make the decision to get rid of those items as soon as possible. It is natural for you to want to take everything plus the kitchen sink, but when practicality strikes, you soon realize your error in judgment. Even on final sections of the AT, I constantly fine-tuned my gear selection, and yes, always sent a few pounds of gear back home after the first week!

Weight is the difference between a good hike and a painful one. I would suggest not carrying more than a quarter of your body weight and, if possible, less than that. You want to go as light as possible without jeopardizing your hike (i.e. make sure you take enough food and warm clothes etc.).

In the next section I am going to share with you the gear Paul, Amber and I have used or currently use and weight is going to be the major factor in determining the gear choices.

Gear

Good quality gear is an absolute essential on the trail. This means not purchasing it at your local super discount store. These stores do come in handy for a multitude of other items you might need for the trip, but don't buy major gear like backpacks, boots, sleeping bags and raingear there. It is best to find a local and knowledgeable Outfitter to obtain this gear from. They usually have everything you need or can get it for you. Remember, these guys and gals not only do this for a living, but most likely they do it for fun. If you get to know these people they are usually big-time outdoor enthusiasts and their day jobs help them get geared up for their trips. They know what they are talking about and can help you make good gear selections based on the trip you are planning and your personal preferences.

Be cautious if you buy your gear online or from a catalog. Yes, you can save some money, but do you know exactly what you are getting? The benefits of a good Outfitter might outweigh the costs you save online. Personally, when it comes to items that require fitting like backpacks, clothes and boots, I would rather try them on in person than risk getting something through the mail that doesn't quite cut it. Since buying online can be a considerable cost advantage, you could find exactly what you need at an Outfitter and then order the same product online. If you do this, please try to support your Outfitter in some other way.

Your gear on the trail is like your house and car at home. It is everything you need to live and commute in the woods, so please do not take it lightly. Research your gear, ask questions, shop around and don't buy until you are completely satisfied. It will save you a lot of money in the long run. Again, like attitude and weight, having good gear is the difference between having a great or a not-so-great hike.

The following pages list a macro view of most of the gear you will need on the trail. I don't go into too much product detail because backpacking gear changes all the time. I want to cover the general gear needed and then you can do additional research to find exactly what kind of pack you want, boots to wear, cook stove to use, etc.

Backpack

I have a Lowe Alpine and Paul and Amber both use Kelty backpacks. All are internal frame packs and are specifically designed for rugged and long distance hiking. Here are some of the differences in our packs.

Amber's Kelty is over two pounds lighter than mine, but she has to carry a lot of her gear—tent, sleeping bag and camp shoes—on the outside of her pack because of the limited internal storage capacity. I made the decision to go with a heavier pack with more internal storage because I like to carry everything inside. Another difference in our packs is the padding and straps. My pack is super comfortable with the weight I carry. If I were to carry the same weight in Amber's pack, the small and narrow hip and shoulder straps wouldn't handle it well and it wouldn't be as comfortable. Believe me, I've tested it.

Another feature difference is Amber's pack has a spot for a hydration reservoir – very common in newer packs; my pack was made before this feature was available.

Manufacturers are producing great packs nowadays and they don't cost an arm and a leg like they did when I started hiking the AT. When purchasing a pack, you really have to have an idea what you want it to do for you. For example, do you want it to have outside pouches for easy convenient access? Compression straps to help compact and centralize your load? Water bottle holders? Hydration system? As mentioned before, my pack predates having an internal pouch for a hydration system, something I want in my next pack. I look forward to the ease of hiking and drinking without having to stop and shed my pack to get a drink of water.

Another major feature you might consider in a pack is an internal or external frame. By far, the majority of backpacks on the AT are internal frames, but you still see the occasional externals. Manufacturers are still making the external frame packs and of better quality than the ones of the old days. I remember well how the old ones used to be out of balance, top heavy and with hardly any padding at all. I can't tell you if the new externals have advantages over internals, because I haven't used one since my days in the Boy Scouts. But the hikers that do sport 'em, seem to be fairly satisfied.

Internal frame packs are the packs of choice. They are lightweight, compact and help distribute weight with a system of pouches and compression straps. I like internals because they are cohesive with your body type. If you get a pack that fits you well, you will hardly notice it is on your back unless, of course, you carry a lot of weight.

The last thing you need to know about buying a pack is making sure it fits you and your body type. Don't make the mistake I did. I bought my pack before I really knew how a pack should fit and where it should rest on my body. Most Outfitters have someone who is good about helping you "fit" a pack. Take advantage of their expertise and benefit from it. Ask a lot of questions and get someone to personally fit you. Also, I highly suggest you fill the pack up with gear (most places let you do this) take a walk around the store and make sure you go up and down the stairs if they have them. Doing this small investigation will give you an immediate feel of whether or not the pack is right for you.

I'm not concerned with telling you what material packs are made of; from what I can tell most backpacks in a quality Outfitter shop are ready to do the job you need it to do on the AT. They are bound together well and use rip resistant materials to take the constant abrasions the woods have to offer. Backpacks can get pricey, but they are worth every penny. Again, this is like your home-away-from-home, so don't cheat yourself here. Do you want something that is going to last the 2180 miles of the trail or something that starts to break down a hundred miles in? I've seen this time and again with people who bring cheap packs on the trail.

Finally, be sure to pick up a pack cover. Backpacks are, at best, water-repellent. If exposed for too long in a rainstorm, your contents can get soaked. A pack cover is a lightweight investment to keep your equipment dry, especially the clothes and sleeping bag you will need when you find shelter! If you do not want to shell out the expense for a pack cover, some hikers put their gear in a heavy-duty trash bag and then stuff it inside their packs to keep it dry.

Footwear

Another important item to carefully consider is footwear. I like to use the car analogy here. You can decide to save a lot of money and buy a cheap car, but you pay the price in durability, comfort, performance and longevity. Or you can spend the extra money and get something that is not only going to last in the long run, but give you the maximum comfort, durability, performance and longevity that is required on the AT.

I am a boot man myself. I have a pair of Asolo's and I wouldn't trade them for anything. Boots, in my opinion, have more durability, traction and support than trail runners. I feel if I wore anything less I could easily break an ankle or stress the hard-working muscles and bones in my feet. Some days I walked over miles and miles of rocks and roots and at days' end my feet were toast. I couldn't imagine what they would have felt like had I worn shoes.

On the other hand, Paul wears a boot/trail runner hybrid. His trail runners give him the support of a boot, but the lightweight feel of a shoe. He didn't always wear these, though. When we first began hiking the AT he had a pair of Montrail boots. They are awesome, but one of the heaviest pair I have ever seen. It didn't take him long to switch to his hybrids. Amber also uses a boot/shoe Vasque hybrid.

Commonly, lightweight boots are the choice of footwear for hikers on the Appalachian Trail, but the last few years I have seen many a thru-hiker wearing cross trainers, trail runners, plain old tennis shoes, and even a few daring it with sport sandals. Most thru-hikers are going through four to five pairs of these during the course of their hike. I, on the other hand, went through two sets of boots before I finally retired them.

It is all about preference and what you are used to. No matter what you decide to wear, make sure you break them in sufficiently before you get on the trail. Be sure they are what you want on your feet for hundreds, and possibly thousands, of miles. The AT is no place to realize your footwear is not right for you – I've seen a lot of nasty hamburger-looking feet on hikers who try to hike big days with new footwear. And, oh, save yourself a lot of heartache and don't buy cheap shoes at the super discount store. The AT eats these for breakfast. They might last a few weeks, if you're lucky.

Lastly, you should definitely consider a pair of lightweight sandals, shoes, or Crocs for camp. After hiking all day your boots can become saturated with sweat, or worse, soaked from creek crossing and wet trail conditions. It is not only a good idea to have camp shoes to allow your boots to dry overnight, but to allow your feet to air out.

A few section hikes ago I decided to cut some weight and left my Waldies (like Crocs) at home. This was a huge mistake and I quickly regretted it. Like the boots, my feet needed airing out and I couldn't do it with my boots on. My only alternative was to go barefoot at camp and it doesn't take much imagination to realize how hard it was keeping my feet clean.

Socks and Liners

Yes, hikers even consider the socks we wear. First of all, don't wear cotton socks, which I will explain in the clothing section. A few good sock choices are Smart Wool and Cool Max – synthetic blends. They help to pull the moisture from your feet to the outside of the socks. The technical term for this process is called wicking. Wicking is a top priority to keeping your feet dry and synthetics wick well!

Visit your Outfitter and I promise they will have several synthetic brands to choose from. Two or Three good pair will be sufficient for your hike, unless you like clean socks every day. It is nice to have clean socks for every day that you hike, but it is not very practical. Most thru-hikers can get away with two or three pairs of socks because they do laundry when they stroll into towns every few days. For me, it can sometimes take up to a week to get to a town. Instead of carrying seven pairs of socks, I choose to wear some pairs more than one day.

Equally important are sock liners. I am so glad I discovered these halfway through my first section hike. Like socks, they too wick moisture, keeping your feet dry. Though the makers don't state it, I have heard liners can help in preventing blisters and I believe it. Anything that helps keep the moisture off your feet is bound to deter foot problems. Off the trail I sometimes still wear a sock/liner combination and other hikers I have spoken with do the same. They are very comfortable and make the experience of wearing socks even more pleasurable. I carry at least two pair of liners.

A word or two on blisters. Here are some tips on how to prevent them.

1) Always keep your feet dry. Not just from rain, but sweat, too. I would periodically stop and take off my boots on the trail to dry my feet and to rearrange my socks (wicking socks work well, but they don't remove all the moisture from your feet).

2) Hot Spots. Whenever you are hiking and feel a hot spot, stop immediately. Take off your boots and assess the situation. Sometimes all it takes is drying your feet and rearranging your socks, but I usually do a quick rub down just to make sure. Before you put your boot back on, look around for any tiny pebbles or twigs inside that might have caused the discomfort. If you do notice a spot that could be a problem, using Mole Skin or a small piece of duct tape is a good preventive measure in my experience.

Earlier in the Introduction I spoke of Amber's determination. On one of our earlier section hikes in Virginia, Amber had a difficult time with blisters. She did everything to prevent the blisters, but they came on with a vengeance. It definitely slowed her down and I really didn't know how she was hiking. One of her feet was very blistered and bleeding. She seriously considered going home, but we decided to take a few days off first to see if they could be revived. We found a hostel and she didn't hike, or barely walk, for a day and a half – all the while caring for her feet. Wouldn't you know, that's all it took? We got back on the trail after a nice cozy break and she was enjoying her hike once again.

Similarly, I had a case of some nasty blisters that resulted from a pair of defective boots I was wearing (unbeknownst to me at the time). I rarely get blisters on the trail, so I was concerned why I got several in the course of three days. On the fourth day I knew why; a few miles into the day's hike the sole of my right boot came off! The boots didn't have many miles on them and were high-end backpacking boots, but were obviously defective. My blisters were a result of the sole tearing away - oblivious to me until it detached completely. I was fortunate to encounter trail magic later that afternoon and caught a ride to get a new pair of boots. The days ahead not only aggravated my existing blisters, but breaking in the new boots caused a few more.

It didn't take long for me to arrive at wit's end. The blisters were too much and I was actually thinking about getting off the trail. But I considered the advice I gave to Amber, and took some time off. I checked into a cheap motel and, for a day and a half, stayed off my feet and treated them every hour or so. When I got back on the trail, the pain wasn't as bad and I could definitely manage it better mentally. I was grateful I decided to rest and didn't take the first bus home. The rest of the hike went well, despite minor uncomfortableness from the blisters.

That is the problem I see with many hikers and their feet problems; they won't stop long enough to care for and give their feet a break. If not dealt with in this manner, many hikers lose several weeks of hiking time or eventually have to get off the trail for good.

3) Boot fit. If your boots don't fit right, you will get blisters. If they are too big I suggest putting on an extra pair of socks for a quick fix, but moisture can build up causing hotspots and eventually blisters. If your boots are too small, all I can say is you are S.O.L. unless you get another pair quick. Again, the best bet is to have a trusty pair of boots or shoes you have already broken in before you get on the AT.

The last bit of advice is to take care of your feet *before* you have problems. Always keep them dry, wear clean socks when you can and give them a massage periodically. Healthy feet are among the top on the list of importance to an enjoyable and successful hike – so much so, I even thank them every now and again!

Sleeping Bags

Sleeping bags are hard to suggest. It all depends on your tolerance and taste. I use a 20-degree mummy bag from The North Face. It's a synthetic bag and was once the lightest on the market for the warmth rating. Easily under three pounds, I decided to carry this bag because if it got wet it would dry quickly. The synthetic fibers can become drenched and bounce back once the bag dries out. Mummy bags are also generally lighter than a standard rectangular-shaped bag, because less material equals less weight.

Another option is a down sleeping bag. They are very warm and lightweight, with one major drawback. They take forever to dry. Plus, a wet down bag's loft is compromised, debilitating its warmth factor – forever!

Some nights my North Face gets a little warm, but there have been times when I have gotten chilled in the middle of summer. It can get cold in the mountains and hollers of the Appalachian Trail, but except for one or two occasions, I've never been out in freezing temperatures. Several nights on the trail I, and Paul—who has the same bag as me—have gotten cold but couldn't understand why because the temperatures were never close to twenty degrees. I have noticed this trend with other brands of temperature-rated bags. On my last section hike in New England, a seasoned hiker imparted some wisdom I found very amusing. His comments were, "A twenty degree bag will keep you alive at twenty degrees, not warm." So true! You may want to take this into consideration if you are buying a sleeping bag specifically for the trail. Buy a bag with a little lower temperature rating, especially if you are hiking in early spring or late fall. Take it from me - freezing all night does not prove for a good hike the following day.

I have sometimes shed some weight by switching to a fleece liner sleeping bag in warmer months. Inevitably, I regret it. There always seems to be one cold, sleepless night that creeps up on me and I swear I will always bring my heavier sleeping bag next time. That is until I hike for a few weeks not needing it, and the day I send it home, it gets cold and I spend half the night chilled and wide awake just waiting for dawn to break so I can get out of bed and hike to warm up.

Sleeping Mats

There wasn't a big selection of sleeping mats to choose from when I started hiking the trail. Until now! I have noticed new brands of mats popping up at Outfitters over the past several years. This is a good thing because they are getting more economical, lighter and a lot more comfortable. Out of the slew of mats available, I used the very reliable and lightweight Ridge Rest mat, until my last section hike of the AT.

Mats are very functional and allow you to sleep in a good degree of comfort and most roll up into a tight bundle. It really comes down to weight again. Nowadays you can get a comfortable, super-lightweight mat, but you will pay the price for it. These mats cost three to four times more than standard foam mats.

Only a few people had air mats when I started hiking the trail, and at the time they were pretty heavy compared to the foam ones. That's all changed in recent years. I have been seeing a greater presence of air mats on the trail, including the popular Therm-a-Rest brand. These mats utilize air to make an even better pad between you and whatever it is you are sleeping on.

If you're like I was, you may think you won't need a mat. You'd better think twice before you get on the AT without one. My first time out I decided I didn't need a mat and soon regretted it. Sleeping on

Mother Earth is not too bad, but sleeping in the shelters night after night can get *hard* to handle – literally! My body loathed sleeping on the hard floors until trail magic produced a mat for me. I will talk about the awesomeness of Trail Magic later in the book.

Clothes

First of all, I don't wear underwear so that is one item I don't have to worry about! As for Paul, he carried three pair and would wash them when he could. Here comes the cotton spiel I promised I would get to. The first important thing Paul and I learned about clothing was to get rid of our cotton clothes! Luckily we were hiking in the summer, if it had been winter the cotton could have easily been deadly. I have nothing personal against cotton. In fact, it is my fabric of choice at home, but it has no place on an extended backpacking trip.

Why do I shun cotton? When it gets wet, it not only feels like you are carrying a brick, it takes forever to dry and you become chilled. Packing cotton clothing has to be the biggest mistake Paul and I made concerning our preparations for the AT. We had all cotton shirts, some cotton shorts, and cotton socks in the very beginning. Imagine this scenario:

You have been hiking all day and your shirt is saturated with sweat. You get to camp and change out of your wet shirt into a dry one. You hang up your shirt hoping it will dry by morning. The next morning no such luck, your shirt is still soaked and you strap this extra pound or so to your pack and start hiking. You reach camp and your other once clean, dry shirt is wet. You now have two soaked cotton shirts. Luckily you have your trusty fleece to change into for the night. The next morning comes and you still have two wet, heavy shirts. So you pick the least saturated and get ready for the chill it will bring. But you are lucky, at least it's not freezing temperatures, then you'd really be SOL.

That's what I know about cotton. Alternatives to cotton? Synthetics, of course. Polypropylene, polyester and countless others are a hiker's dream. They dry quickly whether they are on your body or hanging up. I do admit the cost far exceeds that of cotton, but need I explain why cotton is the not the favored child again? I carry two synthetic shirts and shorts on my section hikes. I used to carry a third set for town visits, but decided long ago it wasn't worth the extra weight.

Other than your socks, liners, shirts and shorts, the only other clothing item you will need is a good fleece pullover. A valuable garment to keep the chill off in the mountain evenings, you can't beat a fleece. It has the two requirements for being hiker worthy; it is lightweight and dries easily. Other than a pair of optional hiker pants, this is it on clothing. Functionality and weight issues are the only considerations, not a desire to make a favorable fashion statement.

Cook Stove

There are tons of products in this area. I will focus primarily on what I've used and what I saw others use. I started out with a Primus Titanium cook stove, not only because it weighs four ounces, but for the ease of setup and cleanup. To setup, all you do is take the stove out of its nifty container, fold it once and then screw it into the fuel canister. Turn the fuel on, ignite it and it is ready to go at whatever temperature you want to cook at. You can adjust the flame instantly with one easy-to-use dial. While I was well into cooking my meal, other hikers were lucky if they even had their stoves primed and up to cooking speed. Another great advantage of this stove is it cleans itself as you cook, leaving no cleanup and virtually no maintenance or upkeep.

My Primus stove uses its own fuel, which is easily found at all Outfitters along the trail. One canister can last two people up to two weeks, depending on how much you cook. A single canister only lasted Paul and I a little over a week one fall trip, mainly because we made a lot of hot chocolate and tea, but also because the base water temperature was close to freezing before we started the boil.

The only thing I have against my stove, and others like it, is the canister waste it produces. I try to be responsible when it comes to the environment and it pains me to know that this canister will help contribute to a landfill somewhere rather than be recycled. I am guilty of convenience like so many others.

One of the most widely used stoves on the AT when I started was, by far, the Whisperlite Multi-fuel. It has a fuel canister, but you can also fill it with a variety of fuels including Coleman fuels and white gas. They can be extremely dangerous for the inexperienced, but they do the job if you know how to use it. Just be careful when you prime it; I have seen many a hiker come close to burning themselves or surrounding areas by letting out too much fuel. It's scary to see a big ball of fire next to a canister with highly flammable liquid in it.

Another cool choice is the ZipStove and other wood stoves. They are powered by a battery-operated fan, use small twigs for fuel and works wonderfully. The only drawback is it's sometimes hard to find dry wood and it would be tough to cook if your battery went dead.

Another popular choice is homemade denatured alcohol stoves made from soda cans. They are extremely lightweight, but the weight comes in carrying the fuel for them. Plus, they take a lot longer to boil water than the first two stoves mentioned.

Lastly, if you are real gung-ho, build a fire for all of your cooking needs! Seriously, I have seen more than a few people who rely on campfires or small fires for all of their cooking or boiling water needs.

Cook Set

Next up is finding a durable cook set. There is only one characteristic I look for in cook sets – weight! I started out using a MSR Titanium set. Now, I use a similar titanium set made by Sno Peak. When Paul and I started hiking we shared one pot between us. That was inconvenient because one of us had to wait till the other was done eating and cleaned up before the other could start cooking. It's a good theory to cut weight when hiking with a partner until you hike twelve miles uphill all day and then decide who gets to eat first when you get to camp! After that first trek of ours, I bought my own pot!

My current cook set comes with a one-liter pot, a half-liter pot, a potholder (pliers) and a skillet that doubles as a lid. You can leave the half-liter pot at home, but bring the rest. Using a lid will greatly reduce the time it takes to boil water, helping you save precious fuel.

Titanium is top of the line and the price is well worth it. It weighs nothing in comparison to the stainless steel alternatives. Stainless steel is good, don't get me wrong; it is durable and gets the job done. I just admire the lightweight Titanium sets compared to the weight of stainless sets. As for aluminum cookware, I would advise against it. For one, it is super easy to burn your food. There have also been reports that you ingest particles of aluminum over time that contribute to heavy metal deposits in your body.

The last two items rounding out your cook set are a spoon and a cup. I use a titanium spoon, but I have seen many of the new-age plastic ones on the trail, too. They are just as light (if not lighter) and seem to do the job as well. Lastly, a cup is an essential for coffee drinkers or for making any other hot drinks like tea and cocoa. I highly suggest these drinks; they are part of the comfort items I will talk about later in the food section. There are few comforts on the trail and hot drinks are one of them. There is nothing like getting up in the morning in the middle of the woods, heating some water for coffee, cocoa or tea and enjoying this treat while you listen to nature wake up around you.

Shelter

I love the tents I have used during my treks on the trail. I started with a Sierra Designs Clip 3 CD weighing about five pounds, which I divided up equally with my hiking partners. For many years it was perfect. It was very easy to setup and kept me dry even in the worst thunderstorms. Plus, the tent was roomy and it offered commendable space for two people, all of our gear and backpacks.

Later on in my section hikes I used tarps, one-person tents, and sometimes didn't take a tent at all! My last trek on the trail I borrowed a friend's MSR Hubba one-person tent. It was fairly lightweight and very easy to setup, plus it was free standing; a feature that came in handy in some areas where using ground stakes wasn't an option. A feature I particularly loved—its vestibule was large enough to cover my pack and boots from the elements.

Another popular shelter idea on the trail is the backpacker's tarp. It is a super lightweight, tough and versatile piece of equipment. You can pitch it anywhere, in several configurations, using tie lines, trees and trekking poles. Because of its weightlessness, many solo hikers carry them. I see the benefits of the tarp, but have one quarrel with them. They don't keep bugs out. I'm not talking about harmless insects, but black flies, mosquitoes, etc. If you can sleep with these things biting you all night, you are a heck of a lot tougher than I am.

One night near Hot Springs, North Carolina, Paul and I thought we would shed some weight and send our tent home, keeping only the rain fly to use like a tarp. That night we set it up with trekking poles and guy lines and reveled in the thought that we had just eliminated a good chunk of weight. Not even an hour later mosquitoes, black flies and a gazillion other no-see-um's began their feast upon us. That was one of the worst nights I have ever had on the Appalachian Trail. There was no sleep for us that night. We literally waited for daylight so we could pack up and get out of there! The next morning we had large red bumps and bites all over us – obviously we lost the battle from the night before. Our tent was in town scheduled to be sent home that day and luckily USPS let us intercept it before it was shipped.

Another tenting option is backpacking hammocks. They are super lightweight and most are like mini-tents, protecting hikers from bugs and rain, but my only qualm with them is you need the perfect space between two good sized trees to erect them.

If you don't want to tent every night you can use the shelters located along the AT. Shelters, or lean-to, as they are sometimes called, are all along the trail from Georgia to Maine. Sometimes they might be as close as three or four miles apart to fifteen miles or more. They can be old log shelters built before the 50s that house about six hikers to fairly new two-story shelters that can accommodate up to twenty hikers.

It's always a good idea to carry a tent even if you plan to use the shelters exclusively. Even the bigger shelters can be packed during the prime thru-hiker season and during inclement weather. Other factors determining shelter availability include; what if the shelter is further than you want to hike in a day? What if you get to a shelter and the water source is unreliable? Thunderstorms tend to fill up shelters quickly, as most hikers don't want to set up their tents in such weather. Lastly, what if you just want to take some solo time away from other hikers?

Having a tent not only gives you options on where you camp, but I guarantee you will experience a full shelter at least once while hiking. It's better to set up a tent in the rain, to have nothing at all.

Water Filters & Containers

Filters are a personal choice. Some hikers won't go without them while others don't think twice about not using them. All I ask is for you to become familiar with the consequences of your choices when it comes to filtering or not filtering water. One word – Giardia!

For many years I carried a Katadyn Combi filter. If you know filters, this one is super heavy compared to any other hiking filter out there, but it was worth it. At the time, this purifier (in my opinion) was by far one of the best on the market. It uses a ceramic element filtering down to .2 micron helping eliminate harmful pathogenic bacteria and protozoa, including giardia and salmonella. It also included activated carbon as a first step to remove chemicals such as gas and farm fertilizers.

Though you can find all these features in other filters too, the main reason I bought this particular purifier is because the ceramic element lasts up to 13,000 gallons in ideal situations. I take ideal as being tap water because on the Appalachian Trail the element life is greatly reduced due to sediment. Paul and I managed to hike over two months before having to change the ceramic element. Theoretically, a solo hiker could use this purifier to hike a substantial portion of the AT with just one filter element. Another added bonus of the filter is it screws directly into Nalgenes and other water bottles, allowing easier water retrieval and pumping.

Pur series filters are widely used on the trail, as are Sweet Water and MSR filters. These filters have a weight advantage, only weighing half of what mine does. The only drawback is their filter cartridge life. They are rated anywhere from sixty to two hundred gallons -- in ideal situations of course. So you can figure on a lot less than that on the trail. What does this mean? It translates to continuously buying replacement cartridges. In the end I guess it depends if you are more worried about saving weight or money. In my experience, I was willing to take on a bit more weight to save a whole lot of money.

One real life story about filters: Paul and I had hiked all of Georgia and were on the early stretch of trail in North Carolina; approximately eighty miles from the start of the AT at Springer Mountain, GA. We met a couple hiking north with a Pur filter. At the 80-mile marker they were already in desperate need of a replacement cartridge. They were at a point where they could barely get a quart of water through their clogged up filter element. In contrast, Paul and I got almost 600 miles on one filter element before having to change it. Remember though, no matter what type of filter you use, you must periodically clean it to extend its life. We would clean our filter element once a day to keep it working efficiently.

These days the water filter selection and technology is amazing. On my last section hike I used a Sawyer one liter water bottle with a built-in filter. All you had to do was fill up the bottle and sip water through the built-in straw. It worked great, if I made sure to keep up with the back flushing maintenance on it. When I didn't, it was hard to get enough water flow through the straw. Nevertheless, I hiked over 700 miles on one filter and at a cost of just over thirty bucks for the bottle and filter it was a great win for me, plus it was the lightest water filtration system I have used to date.

For short trips near good water, you can use iodine tablets or products like Polar Pure or Aqua Mira. Even though the labels warn against prolonged use, I have seen thru-hikers use only these products to treat their water with. I have also seen hikers use Clorox for treating water. Lastly, I have seen other hikers not treat their water at all. I do not condone or encourage this practice because of the obvious hazards, but there have been times on the trail where I encountered water coming straight out of a pipe from underground. Mother earth to me is as good a filter as any. But, just so you know, I have heard stories and met many hikers who have gotten water-related illnesses. Getting Giardia will definitely delay your hike for a while, but at the end of the day your choices affect your hike; make the decision that feels most right to you.

Water containers and bottles are very simple. I carry a one-liter soda bottle and a Nalgene Lexan bottle and sometimes an expandable Platypus. If you are trying to eliminate every ounce of weight you can, use the plastic soda bottles, they work just as well. To tell you the truth, I don't know why so many hikers use Nalgenes. They are great and tough, but soda bottles are thinner and lighter and have lasted as long as I needed them.

Like I mentioned before, there is a rising popularity of packs having an internal pocket for water reservoirs. This is great for hands-free easy access to your water. Finally, for convenience and to save trips to the water hole in the evenings, I carry a water bag for camp use.

Trekking Poles

I cannot stress the benefits of trekking poles enough. Get them; you will be glad you did! When I first started hiking the AT, I used the trusty ole one stick method and thought it was as good as you could get. Then I saw hikers using trekking poles. I didn't understand why and thought it was kind of weird. My exact thought was, "Why are people using ski poles to hike in the mountains?" In time, I finally came to see the light and tried out a pair. WOW! I don't know how I ever hiked without 'em. I will never backpack again without my poles.

Trekking poles feel very natural to me, like an extension of my body. They help me hike better. I can get into a hiking rhythm with poles that I could not do before. It is also physically easier to climb and descend mountains, because the poles offer tremendous leverage benefits. They've saved me from plenty of near falls and helped my overall balance over rough trail. I am convinced the poles even help alleviate stress and impact all over the body, especially in the knees and feet.

Almost every long distance hiker you see on the AT uses trekking poles. The benefits of trekking poles are valuable to users, even beyond physically hiking. You can use your poles to prop up your tarp. You can drive them into the ground and hang your boots to dry. In case of an emergency, you can use them to defend yourself from animals. I don't know of anyone who had to drive away animals, but you always hear hikers jokingly say they would fend off a bear with their poles if they had to!

I still use Garmont trekking poles, but Leki is by far the most widely used pole on the AT that I have seen. Leki are nice, but almost double the cost of mine. My advice to you is to acquire a pair of trekking poles that have the anti-shock feature. This is where I believe poles can really help alleviate impact on the body. Once you have the anti-shock picked out, carefully consider what type of grips you want on them. There are several to choose from – cork, leather, poly, plastic. Choose wisely because these poles will be your companions for many miles. You want something that is going to be comfortable and able to do the job for you.

Rain Gear

All you need is a good waterproof/breathable jacket and pants. Like I mentioned earlier, do not use gear from the local super discount store; I learned the hard way. I used a waterproof parka from one of these stores, but found out real quick it was not breathable. I got just as wet from my own sweat as I would have from the rain. Make sure your jacket is breathable and has plenty of ventilation pockets or zippers.

Depending on where and when you are hiking, there are a slew of jackets to choose from. Brand names usually have jackets for all trail and weather conditions and some of the popular brands I see on the trail are: Kelty, Mountain Hardwear, Sierra Designs, The North Face and Columbia Sportswear. In the long run it is more economical to buy a better jacket starting out, one that has tear-resistant materials. The cheaper jackets do keep you dry, but wear out much sooner. All it takes is one trip through some thick growth and the tears start.

Look for the same features in pants as you do a jacket. Plus, make sure they have a drawstring or Velcro for your waist or else your pants will keep riding low. It is uncomfortable and extremely inefficient to keep stopping to pull up your pants!

Some hikers choose to wear another valuable piece of rain gear called gaiters. Gaiters keep water from running down your legs into your boots during a rain. They also keep your socks dry when you walk through trail that is covered in early morning dew. I haven't seen this done yet, but have often thought of using duct tape to serve the same purpose. That's if are willing to endure the pain of pulling your leg hair out every time you rip it off! Seriously though, I see the value in a good pair of gaiters, but do not wear them myself.

It can get very hot on the trail in certain locations. It is refreshing to get a good dose of cool rain on a hot day of hiking. On the hot days when rainstorms come, I usually take off my shirt and indulge in the coolness of the rain. Once it stops raining, it takes no time to dry off.

Lighting

There are three choices for your lighting needs. A headlamp, a flashlight, or no light. I have experienced all three. Theoretically, if you get everything ready for bed before it gets dark, you will be alright without a light until the middle of the night when nature calls. And that is not a problem, especially if the moon or stars are out. If you don't want to eliminate weight this way, a headlamp is a good idea. It is a hands-free, non-cumbersome, convenient light source. It also comes in handy for the hikers who like to read around bedtime. Make sure you buy a headlamp whose batteries and bulb last. Believe it or not, there are some lamps out there that do not last through two or three evenings of use.

If you're not interested in a headlamp, a great alternative is the Mini Maglite. This sucker is a small, lightweight, tough piece of equipment. Plus it can last a long time on a set of AA batteries. Another option is the key-ring light. You can't use them to read at night, but it is an extremely lightweight back up when you need a bit of light at night for going to the privy or to find something in your pack.

There are so many light choices to choose from, I'll give you this advice. Look at the weight and how long the batteries and bulbs last.

AT Literature & Maps

Most hikers on the trail carry some kind of AT Data Book, trail guide or maps. The majority are updated and published every year. I used the official AT Data Book for many years. This guide is just as important as any other piece of gear you carry on the trail. It is jammed packed with valuable statistics concerning the AT. It lists miles between points all the way to Maine, including towns and shelters. It further details which towns and road crossings have grocery stores, motels, campgrounds or Post Offices nearby. Another important aspect of the data book is it tells you where you can expect to find water. The data book enables you to map your day around water sources and resupply points.

The AT Thru-hikers' Companion is similar to the data book, but goes into much greater detail about the trail and its surrounding areas. It lists motels, hostels, campgrounds, grocers and restaurants, but goes on to give you the costs, hours of operation, where they are located and a phone number. The companion also gives history on points of interest along the trail and basic maps of some of the towns you will cross.

In recent years David "Awol" Miller's AT Guide has been the most popular guidebook I've seen used on the trail. It's a cross between the AT Data Book and the AT Thru-hikers' Companion. I hesitated buying this guide for many years, because I was so used to the Data Book, but I'm glad I finally made the switch. In Miller's guide you will find information you wouldn't find anywhere else; like the location of a trail angel named "Cookie Lady" who gives hikers free cookies and the "Ice Cream Man" Bill Ackerly, who does the same with ice cream. The guide has a lot of information that makes the trail experience even more special.

If you like maps, the ATC has them for the entire Appalachian Trail from Maine to Georgia. They can be a good resource to refer to get an idea of the topography of the mountains and streams. All AT maps now come with elevation profiles (like Awol's guide). Just don't get caught up in the profiles or you will be sadly disappointed – better yet, fooled. Remember, it is very difficult for cartographers to plot every incline, decline, knoll, or ridge on such a small-scale map. I have been fooled many a time by the elevation charts and rarely look at them now.

To paint of clearer picture of what I am talking about, I have the perfect example. I would get to a certain point on the trail and look at my elevation charts to see what type of terrain was ahead. The elevation profile would show two miles of gradual decline. I would slack up mentally, thinking I have two easy miles ahead and around the next bend, run straight into a steep incline. Once I had climbed the mountain and descended, I would run into yet another drastic incline. I guess these elevations were nominal compared to the total distance on the map and they didn't appear on the profile. But they did interrupt my hiking. You have to be in a certain mindset to climb mountains and when you think it will be downhill for two miles, you let up mentally and it is hard to get back into "hill climbing" mode. So if you use these maps, keep hiking step-by-step. Look at the maps for spatial and topographical perspective only, and you will get to your destination in due time.

First Aid Kit

I don't carry much of a first aid kit with me and luckily haven't had any serious injuries or been with other hikers having major incidents. A first aid kit can get heavy in a hurry, so I take the bare essentials. My kit includes a few Band-Aids, a small knife or scissors, and some Tylenol or Ibuprofen. It's not much, but I'm pretty low maintenance and don't need a lot of the extra items you usually find in a kit. Experiment with yours and find out what works best for you. If you don't mind the extra weight, triple antibiotic cream is great for scrapes and cuts, and a small knife comes in handy for a variety of uses.

Stuff Sacks

Stuff sacks are good for keeping everything in your pack organized. I use one for clothes, one for my sleeping bag, a small one for toiletries, one for food, another small one that holds Ziplocs of valuables (credit card, driver's license, cash) and other miscellaneous items. Make sure to use waterproof sacks for your food bag and anything else you want may to hang outside at night.

Toiletries

Fairly straightforward advice here: bring a toothbrush and toothpaste, hairbrush if you like, and don't forget the toilet paper. It is a challenge when you are without!

Depending on the weight you want to subject your back and legs to, I have carried and have seen others carry foot powder, deodorant, razor, lip balm, liquid soap and baby wipes. For women hikers, you have a better idea of what personal hygiene items you need than I do.

Mobile Phones

I didn't carry a mobile phone on the trail until my last section hike from Connecticut to Maine. For years I managed perfectly fine without my cell. When I first started hiking the trail in 2000, it was rare to see a hiker with a cell phone. Obviously, as the years passed, it was rarer to see a hiker without a phone. Just like my switch to using David Miller's trail guide, bringing my cell proved to be a great decision. I was always against being connected on the trail, because I wanted to commune with nature and wanted to limit my distractions. But as we all know, phones, especially smart phones, help in so many ways.

On my last section hike I kept my phone either turned off or in airplane mode most of the time, but it came in handy when I wanted to call a hostel to see if they had availability, check the weather, or order a much needed knee brace that would be waiting for me at the next town. It also eliminated the need for me to tote a heavy camera!

Miscellaneous

Now that you know most of the essential gear you need to successfully hike the AT, these are other items you will need or want to bring:

Journal
Lighter
ID
Cash, credit card or bankcard
Reading material -- book or magazine
Duct tape (several feet can be wrapped around your water bottle)
Trowel (for burying human waste)
Watch
Rope (25 feet give or take for bear bagging)
Bandana or hat
Pocket knife
Camera

Getting to the trail is fairly simple. You can either sweet talk a friend or relative into giving you a ride or, if you are near the AT, there is always an Outfitter or individual who will provide shuttle services, for a fee of course. I would suggest the first choice. Don't get me wrong, shuttle services are great and the people who give them are very interesting - you get some valuable tips on hiking and also hear some good stories they have about other hikers. The reason I like asking family or friends for a ride is because, even after providing them gas and a meal, it is cheaper than a shuttle ride.

How many miles a day should I hike?

A question on all hikers' minds is how far to hike in a day. If you are interested in thru-hiking, the advice I have is for you to get on it! An absolute minimum of fifteen miles per day is what it would take to hike the entire Appalachian Trail in one trip. Anything less and you will be pushing it weather wise. I suggest averaging twenty or more miles a day. Going the extra miles enables you to travel during ideal weather, unless you are one of the few who enjoy cold weather backpacking.

For section hikers, it all depends on how much time you have on the trail and where your ride is going to pick you up. Please, when you are at home planning your trip on the Appalachian Trail, don't start out saying you will do ten or more miles a day. It takes some time to get your body conditioned and you could very well not enjoy what you will go through the first few days if you are hiking long miles. At least give it a few days to a week of single digit hiking before you step it up. Plan your trip accordingly - for your physical and mental wellbeing.

As for me, the long distance section hiker I am, who cares how far I go in a day? As long as I have food and am within comfortable hiking distance to my next resupply point, I don't stress about it. I will give you two examples of how I've hiked the AT over the years. The first example is from my early days of hiking.

If I leave with six days of food on my back and my supply point is fifty-six miles away, I know I must average nine miles a day so I don't run out of food before resupplying. One day I might do seven miles, and another twelve.

Though I like to think I am in control of my hike, I do keep my eyes on my average so I don't fall behind. That first trek on the trail, I didn't try to map out exactly how many miles a day I would hike for the next two months. I knew how much food I was carrying and when I had to resupply. I just didn't like the idea that my next two months were already planned out. It left little room for spontaneity.

Example 2:

On my last section hike of the AT, I was on a schedule to get to Katahdin around a certain day. Despite my early care-free days of hiking without much of an agenda or serious pre-planning, I had to map out my trip in more detail. I knew I had to average around seventeen miles per day to get to Katahdin on time. So I packed my provisions accordingly and carefully planned out resupply options.

When you have decided how many miles you want to hike in a day, you might have the questions, "How do I follow the trail?" and "Will I get lost?" Finding your way on the trail is easy. You will be guided by white blazes painted on the trees (around eye level) periodically. All you have to do is follow these and you will be A-OK. You will come across Blue blazes, also. These usually indicate a water source and/or side trails. Do yourself a favor and take a few of these side trails, they are some of the most spectacular places you will see along the AT. Most of the ones Paul and I took were less than two miles roundtrip and proved to be well worth it.

Please note: whenever I do a blue blazed trail, I always start back on the AT where I left off. There is a word for hikers who hike every single step of the trail, they are called Purists. I'm not going to say I am a hardcore purist. I have missed a few feet here and there. For example, when you cut off trail to a shelter or campsite, there are usually two paths leading back to the AT, one going north and the other south. I don't always bother to hike the same path out I came in on. I sometimes take the one that gets me in the direction I need to go.

In all honesty, I probably only miss a few yards of the AT doing this, but it could add up if a hiker did it at every shelter along the trail. There are varying levels of Purists on the trail. At the top are the hikers who hike every single step of the path, never missing a white blaze. On the other hand, I've seen hikers take every blue blaze shortcut they could find!

Sometimes Purists criticize those who use blue blaze trails as shortcuts. I cannot criticize those hikers because, like I have said many times already, we have to hike our own hike no matter what others are doing. If hikers want to take shortcuts or catch rides, that is their hike, their business. Don't worry about what others are doing; be content with your hike. Don't be too rigid; change your plans in the middle if that's what happens!

Many looped side trails are worth every step. If you get a chance, take the time to hike Raven Rock Cliffs trail near Muskrat Creek Shelter, which is close to the borders of North Carolina and Georgia. And don't forget to visit Wasilik Trail, not too far north from Raven Rock Cliffs and just before you get to Rainbow Springs Campground. Wasilik is the site of the second largest poplar tree in the United States. It is truly an awesome spectacle of nature! In fact, both of these places are beyond description. You must see them in person to fully experience the beauty they have to offer. I hiked both of these after officially finishing my AT miles for the day. Yeah, sometimes you can find more miles in you to see these places, especially early on in the trail. But even my day-by-day style of hiking started to erode the farther north I got. The time I got to spend on the trail was less and less and I found myself sticking to the white blazes mostly, only going on .2 or .3 side trails occasionally.

Water

Water is life. Make sure you drink plenty of it on the trail. The first thing I do before starting the days hike is "camel up". I borrowed this term from some hikers ("Stumble Feet" and "Insomniac", both coal miners) Paul and I met in Tennessee. "Camel up" means what it says. We would drink at least a quart of water, often more, before we started hiking for the day to help us stay hydrated. I carry one or two quarts with me and fill up whenever I find good water source. I usually "Camel up" before leaving any water source unless I know I will be hiking in an area with plenty more reliable sources.

Dehydration can and does happen on the trail if you don't drink plenty of water. It is easy to forget to drink water on a section of easy trail. I stress to you, even if you do not feel thirsty, sip on water throughout the day. Another helpful hint is to carry at least a quart of water with you at all times, Paul and I learned the hard way.

We were hiking a section of trail and decided not to carry extra water so we could shed a few pounds. The hiking got tough and it got rather hot that day. We soon ran out of water. We kept hoping a source would come, but none did. We hiked miles before we found water. Dehydration sucks! I began to get cottonmouth, light headed, nauseous, dizzy and was even having mild hallucinations. By that time I was getting a little scared and was dying of thirst. Being in the middle of the forest, the only thing we could do was to keep hiking and hope water would turn up soon.

We finally found water and that first drink was the best feeling! On the first drink I could feel the life coming back into me. Don't let this happen to you. Stay hydrated and carry at least a quart of water at all times. I wished I could say I learned my lesson from that experience, but on another hike in a particularly dry section of Pennsylvania, it happened again. I literally thought I was going to die of thirst! Since the second experience, I ALWAYS carry at least a liter of water at all times.

The AT trail guides will tell you exactly where water is on the trail, but be cautious because some sources can be a small muddy puddle or worse – seasonal and completely dried up when you get there. So it is best to fill up every time you see a plentiful, clean, water source.

Overall, the water situation on the trail is pretty good and some of the best I have ever had. No chemicals and compounds like chlorine, lead or fluoride, just filtered clean and cold by trusty Mother Nature. As I mentioned earlier, whether you treat your water is entirely your own choice, just remember you are taking a dangerous risk.

Lastly, it would be wise to invest in a water bag. I promise it will save you many unnecessary walks to the water hole at the end of the day. You tend to use a lot of water in cooking and cleanup at camp. If you fill your water bag up when you get to camp, you will probably have enough for all evening and breakfast the next morning.

You will see what I am talking about when you get on the AT. Nothing is worse than hiking all day and then having to hike to the water source several times in one evening. Sometimes the water sources are level walking and not far away, but other times you might have to hike a good distance down a mountain and back up. Do this two or three times in one night and you will be ready for a water bag, too!

Shelters

Shelters are located along the entire AT. They can be as close as a few miles apart to as far away as fifteen miles or more. Most shelters are single decks that hold around eight people, more if it is raining; no hiker wants to see another have to pitch a tent in the rain and usually makes room for them. There are some shelters that have an upper deck or loft, expanding the capacity by six or eight spaces. Those who reach a shelter after its capacity is maxed out, either have to hike to the next one or pitch a tent.

You can usually find space in a shelter unless it is prime thru-hiking season, which is late March, all of April, and as late as the first week of May for North bounders. Also, many shelters have a picnic table for cooking and gathering, and an outhouse nearby.

I can't leave the subject of shelters without telling you about mice. Mice are synonymous with AT shelters. As soon as it gets dark, they emerge, ready for a snack! I have plenty of mice stories. One time a mouse got into my food bag and took a bite out of my king-sized Snickers bar. I was heartbroken, but not angry. It was a learning experience I had to go through. Another time one spent all night making a nest in my backpack out of newspaper. I have no idea where she got the newspaper!

I remember the first time Paul and I encountered a mouse on the AT. It was our very first night sleeping in the shelter on Springer Mountain, Georgia. It was dark and we were lying in our sleeping bags talking when all of a sudden a mouse used Paul's head and sleeping bag as a racetrack. The mouse ran over Paul's head and all the way down his sleeping bag before jumping back onto the wall. Startled, Paul made a hilarious scream and got our neighbors wondering what was going on. I admit this mouse was a daredevil; they usually don't get so personal.

Mainly mice are more of a conversation piece and a good laugh for hikers. If you secure your gear properly, they aren't a menace at all, just amusing critters running around all night. I just want you to be aware of mice and take notice. They will make themselves at home in your stuff if you don't secure it properly. So make sure you cinch your pack tightly and hang your food bag up before going to bed.

A quick note on hanging food bags. There are normally "mouse proof" ropes provided in the shelters to hang your food bag on, but they don't always work. On more than one occasion I have seen mice maneuver around them. Hang your food bag upside down with the opening on the bottom. In this case, if the mice are acrobatic enough to get on your bag they won't be able to scale down the side to get into the opening.

Mail Drops vs. Town Resupply

Mail drops have always been my preferred method of resupplying. They are fairly convenient and can save you a lot of money in the long run. When you're at home planning your hike, you have the opportunity to stock up on supplies gradually. You have the freedom to watch for sales and even to visit local bulk food retailers, like Sam's Club and Costco.

Saving money is good, but convenience is the greatest aspect of preparing your food supplies at home. You have everything you need in one location, ready to be distributed. There you can breakdown, sort out and package the food for each section of the trip. Remember, though, doing it this way you have to have a hiking plan ready – how many days of food you will carry and where to send the packages to and when. Most trail guides list all the Post Offices close to the trail with their zip codes. The A.W.O.L. guide is good about showing the hours of operation, which is very important. I will explain why in just a minute.

For mail drops, all you have to do is send it addressed to yourself c/o General Delivery with the town and zip code. For good measure I like to add, "Hold for AT Hiker."

Look at your guide and try to send your mail drops to the post offices closest to the trail, usually within zero to three miles. If you are not careful you might send it to a post office that is thirteen miles away and that can be a difficult hitch, depending on the area.

An alternative is to send your mail drops to hostels on the trail. Most hostels like for you to stay the night in return for them holding your package. This is a great way to support hostel owners, most of which aren't getting rich off hiker stays, but are truly passionate and excited about hosting hikers.

Mail Drops work well for me, but for thru-hikers there is one major difference. Since they hike a lot more miles in a day than I do, they have to be very prudent in getting their packages sent ahead of time, often two or three at once. Thru-hikers might only carry three days of food and don't have the freedom to wait around a day if their package hasn't arrived on schedule. What if they get to the post office after it closes or on a Sunday? That's why if you plan on thru-hiking, it is best to have multiple food drop packages sent ahead, to make sure they will be at the destination *before* you arrive. I've seen several hikers delayed because of a food drop that didn't arrive on time. Their only solution was to camp out and wait for their package to arrive, or have it forwarded to another town farther north and try resupplying at the local convenience or grocery store.

Here's a helpful tip: if you send yourself boxes via the USPS, use Priority shipping. If you get in a situation where you need to forward the box to another location on the trail, it is free. If you don't use Priority shipping, you have to pay to ship the box again.

If you go the route of mail dropping, be diligent about mixing up the foods in your packages. You will thank me later because there is nothing as disheartening as getting the exact same food in the mail that you just got finished with the week before. Of course, you'll still have the same staple items, but you can mix it up enough to make it interesting. Even better, if you know someone who will package your food on call, you can ring him or her up and tell them exactly what your taste might be for the next drop.

On our first hike, Paul and I followed two hikers that got the same foods every mail drop. They got so sick of the exact same foods they gave a lot of it away. We were lucky to be in the right place at the right time. We got all kinds of goodies, but we usually traded something of equal value. That's another cool thing about the trail…there is always a lot of trading and bartering going on with food. So it might be of interest to you to carry the occasional "high valued" items, it will give you more bargaining power!

Not all hikers have the support system to effectively have mail drops, so they must shop at towns on or near the trail. This is nice, but can get expensive and you don't always run across a big grocer. Sometimes you might be shopping in a little trading post, scrounging for enough rations to last a week. This can be difficult unless you can live on candy bars, beef jerky and Pop Tarts. My experience has been that most trail towns are receptive to hikers and have a small section of trail food for us, with a markup, understandably.

Although I rely mostly on mail drops, I do occasionally restock in town; mostly to supplement or extend my rations until I reach a post office. Plan your food resupply logistics seriously and your hike will go smoothly.

Towns

Here is the part where special, clean, just-for-town clothes come in handy that I spoke about awhile back. It is not a prerequisite, but it definitely can't hurt your chances on getting a ride. Getting to towns is fairly easy. Generally you will hike off of the trail onto a hardtop road. According to your guide, you will either turn right or left (trail guides usually use N, S, E, & W) and immediately stick your thumb out. You have the option of walking to town, but I don't know many hikers who do. I admit the first time you stick your thumb out is weird if you're not used to hitchhiking, but you soon get used to it, good at it, and I would go as far to say you will enjoy it.

Hitchhiking is a way of life for hikers, so don't worry about it. You will always get a ride, though sometimes it could take a while. The key is to be patient and smiling definitely helps. I enjoy hitchhiking because of the people you meet and the conversations you have. If someone picks you up, they most likely have picked up other hikers and are used to it. Don't be afraid of the people picking you up. Most are locals and know the "trail people" or "hikers" come through and enjoy offering their time for a good cause. Here is where your clean clothes play a role. You attract a ride because you look clean and the driver knows you are not going to soil his seats! You still stink of course, but not nearly as bad. The same goes for the town. People know we are AT hikers, but I don't want to prove it with my smell if I can help it, especially if I want to go into a semi-nice restaurant and get a good meal.

In my eyes, visiting towns is a mixed blessing. On one hand, it is nice to get a shower, do some laundry, get something to eat at a local restaurant, have some ice cream, and see a different regional culture. But here is where extremes start surfacing. I have been in the woods for a while…very at peace and mellowed out, breathing good air, enjoying the silence and sounds of nature. In contrast, everything in town seems to be too fast and not natural at all. The first thing you smell are chemical pollutants like car emissions and lawnmower fumes. Everybody seems to be in a hurry, not stopping to admire the beautiful day or striking up conversations. It's just the "natural" societal hustle most of us left before spending 24/7 communing with nature. I often find myself out of my element and wanting to get back on the trail as soon as possible - usually after all of my errands are done, my belly is full and I've had a chance to find some ice cream!

I rarely stayed in a hotel or hostel on most of my section hikes (except the last one). At the time, my observations of other hikers were that many stayed at a hotel or hostel for the night so they could get everything possible out of the town visit; restaurants, bars, laundry, etc. When Paul and I hiked our first section and even when Amber and I hiked Virginia to PA, I had only stayed at one motel and a handful of hostels over those 1000+ miles. I had nothing against motels and hostels, but at the time couldn't justify the cost of a room for one night when I could hike back in the woods and sleep for free!

That all changed on my last section hike. I found myself visiting a hostel about once a week. Money wasn't really an issue and I enjoyed the time off the trail to do a lot of personal maintenance. Taking time off to rest, shower, eat good meals, and indulge in Ben and Jerry's was where I was at that point in my life. Also, hostels are a great gathering place for hikers and I met some folks I am still in touch with today.

If you don't stay in hostels and motels, you can usually find a place to take a shower and do laundry for a nominal fee. The most prevalent places are gas stations, truck stops, and campgrounds. Again, the A.W.O.L. guide does an excellent job of listing all of this information.

Other Hikers

Meeting other hikers is one of the best fringe benefits of hiking the Appalachian Trail. I have met many good people on the trail. It is very easy to experience a deep kinship or bond with other hikers on the trail. It never ceases to amaze me how this is true every time I get an opportunity to do a section hike. The trail just attracts very kindred spirits; a few weirdos, too, but mostly kindred spirits. This was especially meaningful, because in my normal life these encounters happened only rarely, until I moved to the awesome part of the country I live in today!

If you hike any kind of distance at all, you will meet up with many hikers you could call close friends. Hiking together creates special bonds. It makes me think of what being in a clan would have felt like if I lived in ancient times. We each have our individuality, but the interaction of individuals as a group makes life what it is. It is these moments of connection that elevates the trail experience to an even higher level. Enjoy the connections while you can, because the time will come when a hiker moves on. It is difficult to say goodbye to your new friends, but we are each out there for different reasons and we have to hike our own hike. Don't fret. Inevitably there will be a new set of hikers you will meet and build relationships with. I still correspond with many of my trail friends to this day.

The Appalachian Trail offers diversity, yet equality among its hikers. To expand further on the diversity of the hikers, I'll relay some of the vocations of the people I have encountered. I've met carpenters, website designers, computer consultants, software development techs, coal miners, a pizza delivery guy, a tax accountant, teachers, salespeople, executives, small business owners, a writer, a mail carrier, priests, college students, boy scouts, drifters, a bartender and one of his faithful patrons, and even two retired VPs from a major brewing company. It is awesome to see such a variety of people hiking and socializing along the trail. We have the AT in common no matter where we are from, what our position in society is, or what color our skin might be.

It is amazing how well hikers get along. Everyone is happy, courteous, intuitive, and polite (well, most people!). Out of everyone I have encountered on the trail, I have met one person who seemed potentially dangerous. One hiker out of hundreds, possibly a thousand or more, gave me the impression of being dangerous. Even at that, this guy was funny and likeable. He just had something about him that was unsettling to me. So put any fear or rumors you have heard about the Appalachian Trail being dangerous, to rest. There are literally millions of people on some part of the AT each year (usually National Park Lands) and since its inception in 1923, there have only been a handful of deaths. There is no comparing the crime rate on the trail to that of any town in the U.S. for the same period of time.

Now that you know the AT is safe, I have to briefly mention women hikers. You go girls! Women are no exception to hiking the trail. Yes, the majority of hikers are men, but the women I've seen on the trail are super tough and a great percentage of them were thru-hiking. They can put on the miles and definitely carry the weight as well as a man. Paul and I saw a woman one summer who was carrying a pack that looked as heavy as both of ours combined! We were stunned and couldn't believe it. She even beat us to the first major resupply point on the AT. She made it, but got smart and we saw her sending a bunch of her gear home.

Though many women start out solo, they usually team up with a partner or two as they hike the great trail. Or, they have a big dog. This helps keep every young, drooling male hiker at bay. These young men are pretty harmless, but I guess I wouldn't feel comfortable if I were a woman surrounded by a bunch of men who have been out in the woods for weeks and months at a time.

Weekend and day hikers use the Appalachian Trail, also. They ask a lot of questions of thru-hikers and are enthusiastic about your hike -- some even envious. Be good to them, they give you food! Seriously, they are great people. A nice atmospheric change of pace and attitude. They are out enjoying what precious time they have on the trail and their vibrant, fresh attitudes rub off. Since they are only out for a few days, they like to build fires (It is rare to see thru-hikers building a fire, most go to bed when it gets dark) and this can be a good time of stimulating conversation if you decide to partake.

It is refreshing to see day hikers, too. Sometimes it is easy to take the trail for granted and lose some of the experience of it. Seeing day hikers out enjoying every second, helped me realize I needed to be more grateful for each day I spend on the Appalachian Trail. There are many people who want to do what I've done, but can't because of family or work obligations.

Don't let me scare you off talking about all the people on the AT, because it is far from overcrowded. There is a nice balance of interaction. Some days you might not see a single hiker, but other days you could see a dozen or more. I like to socialize but, like most hikers, I need quiet time to myself, too. To ensure this, I often find a nice place to pitch my tent rather than stay at a shelter. When I am ready to interact more, I start sleeping in shelters again.

Enjoy and cherish the relationships you build on the trail. Even though they are not the motivation to go out and hike over 2000 miles, it is a sweet by-product. Trail friends increase the joy of the AT tremendously.

Pets

Pets are permitted on most of the Appalachian Trail. I only know of a few places they aren't allowed and that is in the Smoky Mountains National Park, White Mountains of New Hampshire and Baxter State Park in Maine. There may be a few other places that don't allow pets, so be sure to check your trail guide before setting out. The trail guides are also pretty good at listing kennel and pet shuttle services for hikers. For instance, I know there was a place near the Smokies where someone would pick up your dog, house it for the week, and deliver him/her to the trail once you made it through the Smokies.

For the most part, every dog I saw was very suited for the trail. There are some exceptions, but for the most part they could walk the miles and the terrain didn't affect their paws too much. Most were very friendly to humans and other dogs, but occasionally I would run into a hiker with a dog that didn't like other dogs. Most owners were considerate and either kept their dogs on a leash or camped separately from other dogs.

If your dog gets chase crazy when they encounter squirrels, deer or other wildlife, you should plan to keep them on a leash or consider leaving them at home. I have met many hikers that have spent some serious time looking for deer chase crazed dogs. And, often times, when the dogs return, they have lost their packs! If you didn't already know, there are small packs made especially for dogs. They are roomy enough to carry their food and a collapsible water bowl.

Other considerations for pet owners are: respecting other hikers, hitchhiking with a dog, and visiting motels/hostels and restaurants. First, please respect other hikers' space while on the trail. Don't take up valuable shelter space for your pet if a human hiker needs it. Also, be considerate when hikers are eating – some do not like begging dogs during dinner time.

When it comes to hitchhiking, I've heard a few accounts of it being harder to catch a ride with a dog. You never know what type of vehicle is going to pick you up and sometimes there is barely enough room for a hiker and his/her pack. Adding a furry friend might be asking a bit too much from people. On the other hand, I think maybe their chances aren't necessarily decreased. Wouldn't fellow dog lovers be more apt to pick up a hiker with a dog?

Motels and hostels that accept dogs are hit and miss. When you do find one, expect to pay an upcharge. Lastly, there is always the question of what to do with your dog when it's time to go into a grocery store or restaurant.

Wildlife

Lions and tigers and bears, oh my! I seriously doubt you will see the first two of these animals on the AT, but you could see the latter. Bear stories are everywhere on the trail, either straight from hikers or by written accounts in the shelter logbooks. We met two brothers from Mississippi hiking the Smoky Mountains section of the AT who told us about their bear encounter. They came into view of a bear some distance up trail and when it saw them it started walking their way. That was all they needed. They got spooked, turned around and ran a half mile back down trail with their packs on! We saw them that evening and they were still wired.

Another reported encounter was with a female hiker friend of ours. She was cooking a meal and, luckily, in close proximity to the fenced shelters they have in the Smokies. A bear came investigating the smell and she ran into the shelter and closed the gate. She told us the bear hung around for quite a while, even though she was yelling and banging on the fence. I guess whatever she was cooking was very tempting to our furry friend.

Almost always, the stories of bear encounters have been harmless. Generally speaking, bears are just as afraid of us as we are of them. But since bears are getting used to seeing us and like the smell of the food we carry, I hear they are not as shy as they used to be. Just be cautious if you encounter one. If things got hairy, my first inclination would be to run or climb a tree -- too bad the bear can do both better than me! Some experts say to play dead, others say to scream, wave your arms and look as threatening as you possibly can. All of my bear sightings, except two, have been watching the rear end of the bear as it runs away after seeing or hearing me!

Other animals you might witness on the AT are plenty of deer, from big bucks to yearlings, moose, tons of squirrels, chipmunks, woodpeckers, turkey vultures, hawks and all the birds you care to identify. Just lately I have become interested in the wonderful world of bird watching. I haven't gotten to the stage of buying the books and learning their Latin names yet, but I do enjoy sitting quietly and watching them interact with each other and go about building nests and hunting for food. I read in a logbook at a shelter in Tennessee, about a whippoorwill that would wake hikers up in the early hours of the morning before the sun rose. Sure enough, the next morning I awoke to the beautiful song of my little friend. Grouse and flocks of wild turkey are other birds you will see on the trail.

I heard coyotes in the Smokies, but never caught a glimpse of one. I also saw signs of rooting made by wild boars. The Smoky Mountains are so overpopulated with wild boars, I've heard they actually have a person go in and shoot them to lessen their numbers. I heard they pull them out of sight and let the predators eat them rather than taking them out. My vote would be to have a big barbeque for hungry hikers, man that would be a feast!

If you are a reptile buff, you can easily find salamanders and lizards around any water source. For the first half of the trail, snake sighting weren't very prevalent for me. I didn't see my first rattlesnake until Pennsylvania, and the darn thing wouldn't move out of the trail so I could go around it. To round out the world of critters, I have seen insects of all kinds, grubs, ground hogs, raccoons, skunks, owls, wild ponies (in Grayson Highlands) and porcupines.

Views & Scenery

Sometimes I get so caught up in hiking the trail that the beauty fades away and trees become "just trees" to me. When this happens and I become aware of my digression, I immediately snap out of it and appreciate what I am looking at and have the good fortune to be around.

The Appalachian Trail has some of the most beautiful scenery I've had the opportunity to lay my eyes upon. When I find myself looking at "just" another tree I change my perception and notice the beauty again. Being able to see the inner workings of nature and the interrelatedness to the rest of the world, is an awe-inspiring moment. The AT's beauty is incredible…from the lowest valleys to the highest mountain summits. The balds and ridge tops are awesome! Some days you see clearly for miles. In the distance you might see nothing but forest and other times you will see farms or even a city dotting the landscape. You can also be passing over a bald on a dreary, foggy day and barely see a few feet in front of you. Since spectacular views are few and far apart, don't miss out on the precious vistas. I have often thought of going back someday and revisiting the views I missed due to inclement weather.

Balds and ridge tops and the occasional break in the trees provide a great place to take a break and soak it all in. I regret the moments I have not taken the time to fully experience some of the vistas I encountered. It only takes a minute to relax your pace and enjoy the fantastic scenery. When I stop to do this, that is when the moment grabs me and the beauty and peace really hit me. Be sure to bring a camera for all the great photo treasures waiting for you!

The other end of the spectrum of views and scenery is the night sky. If you are lucky enough to camp in a clearing, you will have a nice treat. The stars on the AT are the brightest and most abundant I have seen away from the lights and glow of the city. I know very few constellations, but it would be an astronomer's dream. The moon is always a sight to cherish since you don't always get a clear look at it through the treetops. Sunsets are equally beautiful, no matter where you are on the trail.

Leave No Trace

I first learned of the LNT principles when I was in Boy Scouts. I had no idea at the time that it was a legitimate non-profit organization based out of Colorado. I thought it was something my Scoutmaster came up with to better serve the environment. I strongly agree with LNT and hope you will practice it diligently on the trail. Without observing these basic guidelines, the Appalachian Trail could quickly go from being pristine and clean, to nasty and trashy.

The LNT principles are:

> Plan ahead and prepare
> Travel and camp on durable surfaces
> Dispose of waste properly
> Leave what you find
> Minimize campfire impacts
> Respect wildlife
> Be considerate of other visitors

The principles speak for themselves, but I feel I must elaborate on one. Disposing of human waste properly on the AT is very important. There are millions of people on some part of the trail each year; most near the National Parks, Forests and Natural Areas, but there are still thousands of people hiking various sections throughout the 2,100 plus miles of the trail. Please use the privies located at most shelters. If there is not a privy, make sure you carry a trowel to bury your human waste with. Respect other hikers and the trail by burying your waste. It sucks to be around a shelter without a Privy and have to follow the "Pee" trail to use the bathroom. First, it can stink badly and second, you have to really watch where you step! Please be respectful and take the time to dig a small cat hole and dispose of your waste properly. Hikers generally do well in this area, but I have run into a few bad spots where it is like walking onto a mine field. It's not so bad in the daylight, but watch out when it gets dark! And remember another thing, LNT asks that you carry out your toilet paper. It is an eyesore to see TP strung everywhere. Personally, I choose to bury it rather than tote it around.

Leave No Trace, Inc. goes more in depth with all of the above principles. To learn more about the Leave No Trace Organization, refer to the Appendix section in the back of this book.

Food

Now that you know what to expect on the AT and what gear to take, let's look at the food side of it. As you saw in the gear section, everything you take on the trail is essential to your comfort and/or wellbeing. Gear is important, but food is that, times some. Bottom line—you need the fuel to carry you the miles. This is the area where I still carry too much weight, but it's worth it to me.

It is not just a question of eating, but eating well. When planning your food, a helpful hint is to remember that you will be consuming a lot more calories the longer you are on the trail. When you start hiking double digit miles day after day, your body will demand more and more calories to keep up.

You can always recognize a thru-hiker or long distance section hiker because they're always hungry and, when you do see them, they will likely be snacking. If you are a weekend hiker, be careful. I have seen some thru-hikers who practically beg for your leftovers! It's true. Every time I am on a section hike, I reach an insatiable appetite. Don't let this scare you, it is manageable. Just try and keep from eating your whole week's rations at once. To ensure this, make sure you bring plenty of high calorie snack items. You will need these constantly to keep your energy up.

To Cook or Not to Cook

Your trip, it is totally up to you. Here is what I think. Both! And really, it depends on how long you are out for. One positive to not cooking is you don't have to carry the weight of the stove, fuel and cook set; but if you are out for any extended period of time, cold foods get old fast. Plus, I'm not entirely convinced this will help save weight in the long run. I've seen people who don't cook and some of the food items they carry look like they weigh more than if they took a stove and the common trail entrees most hikers use. It's also very satisfying having a nice hot meal at the end of a long day of hiking. I've seen more than one hiker who don't use stoves, drool over other hikers' meals!

What Kind of Food and How Much

The never-ending question. After years of hiking the trail, I am still coming up with new food ideas and how to rotate them into my regime. I also still experiment with how many days of rations to carry at once. What follows is a description of the foods I carry or have carried in the past.

Breakfast

Instant oatmeal is my main breakfast staple. Half the time I don't even boil water for it. I just put it in a cup of water, mix it and drink it. To switch it up, sometimes I take dry cereal with instant milk, but this never seems to fill me up and I find myself stopping for lunch or a snack not long after leaving camp. Lately, I've switched to granola cereal. It's a little on the heavy side, but it's a way I treat myself on the first few mornings after I pick up a food drop. Plus it really sticks with me for several hours of morning hiking.

On lazy mornings when I don't feel like messing with oatmeal or cereal, I eat some GORP, a bagel, or a protein or breakfast bar. If I do this, I am usually eating an early lunch because a few hundred calories won't get you far.

Believe it or not, that is it on breakfast items and I do not have any alternatives on deck right now. I did try making pancakes a time or two, but they never turned out like I expected, so I quit carrying the mix.

Lunch

Filling lunch items can be a bagel or a soft tortilla shell covered with peanut butter or a chunk of cheese. Sardines or tuna (any prepackaged fish in lightweight sealed packs) with crackers or another carb can be good and filling, too. A favorite lunch item of mine in the early days, were MRE (meals-ready-to-eat) entrees. They can be a bit heavy, but are very filling and are jam-packed with calories and nutrition. While at home packing for the trail, I took them out of their big packages to help reduce the weight. They are substantially cheaper if you buy them in bulk. I would usually buy a case of mixed entrées in flavors like turkey breast, chicken in shells, pasta with vegetables, red beans and rice and the list goes on. Have one of these for lunch and it will likely hold you over for a while.

Dinner

I cook a Lipton Noodle, Pasta or Rice dinner almost every evening on the trail. These are the norm for many other hikers' evening meals, too. Sometimes I put a can of tuna in the noodles to get a protein fix. Tuna is an item you won't see many hikers carry because of the weight, but it is worth it to me for the protein. It is hard to get necessary protein while on the trail because the majority of the food we carry is high in carbohydrates. And like I said earlier, it's becoming easier to find packaged fish and meat (like summer sausage or pepperoni) these days, so I always carry a few of these to add to my lunch or dinners for the week.

Other dinner items include shells and cheese, macaroni and cheese and other pasta and cheese dinners. Like granola, this is a treat for me, but too heavy to carry long, so I usually eat it the first night after I pick up my food shipment. To me, cheese on the trail is like liquid gold. I can't get enough of it!

Other meal ideas for dinner are the universal ramen noodles. Good for broke college students and hikers alike! But you won't survive on these alone. It's good to carry some 'fillers' in your food bag for ramen nights. I carry dehydrated soups and veges for these occasions. My good friend would always send me on the trail with a big bag of veges she dehydrated herself. Her mix was better than anything you could ever buy. The mix included mushrooms, peppers, greens, carrots, beets, and on and on!

Another recommendation for dinner is instant mashed potatoes. Alone they are great because they have a lot of flavors to choose from, but I would often add dehydrated veges to liven up the meal.

I sometimes carry a few ounces of olive oil to add to my meals. If you look at the label on olive oil, it is loaded with calories. For its weight, I would say it has more calories per ounce than most snacks. I once heard a hiker mention he carries olive oil during winter hikes and he takes a big swig every now and again to help keep his energy up.

When I first started hiking the trail, Lipton (or Kerns) noodle dishes were the dominant dinner of choice for most hikers. That was the case for much of the fourteen years it took me to hike the AT. Some hikers carry these meals exclusively; and I have to say they have gotten a lot better in taste over the years, too! They are inexpensive, lightweight, tasty, and packed with calories.

I can't end this section without mentioning the commercial brand dehydrated meals. Mountain House and Backpacker's Pantry are the most popular, but there are a handful of other brands including PackitGourmet. These dehydrated meals taste great and are super lightweight, but the biggest drawback for a long distance hiker is cost. These meals can cost well over six times more than Lipton meals. They are fine for a weekend hike, but spending this kind of money every day for weeks or months at a time isn't cost effective. One positive, the meals are big enough to share with a friend. If you are hiking with a partner, the cost of one of these might only be a few dollars more than Lipton meals per person.

A last bit of advice on dinner before I end with a story about an interesting hiker and her food. Don't carry anything that takes more than ten minutes to cook. If you go with beans and rice meals or pasta meals, you are talking sixteen, eighteen, twenty minutes to cook. These can quickly wreak havoc on your stove's fuel consumption. If you only carry a few days of food at a time, it would work. But, anything more than that and you will be cutting it real close fuel wise. Besides, the less time you are cooking meals, the less fuel you have to carry and the less weight on your back.

Now to the story of a hiker Paul and I met just before Hot Springs, North Carolina. She was a sixty-six year old missionary from Zimbabwe visiting a friend here in the states and had always wanted to hike a section of the Appalachian Trail. This woman was tough! She had an old, worn backpack practically exploding from all the gear she was carrying. I would guess the pack weighed at least fifty-five pounds. She did her laundry on the trail and cooked all her meals over an open fire. Here is the part I liked…she cooked real food! The night we first met her she was making a stew and I saw carrots, celery and potatoes being put into her pot. Wow! Now that is the way to cook on the trail if you want to carry the weight. After dinner was completed and just before it got dark, she made up a batch of tea complete with honey and cream. She offered and we could not refuse.

We saw her leave early the next morning using a mountain ice pick as a trekking pole. She was truly a sight to see. I admire how she came to the trail on her on terms and made her dream come true. Her style was not shaken in the least with all of us modern, high-tech gearhead, synthetic clothes-wearing hikers around her. We never met up again but did keep track of her in the shelter journals. After that encounter, Paul and I were inspired and would try to buy some fresh veggies on our town trips and make a stew the same evening as not to carry the heavy vegetables for more miles than we had to. It was easier to carry the weight in our stomachs than on our backs!

Desserts & Snacks

Now to the good part! I always carry plenty of snacks -- maybe too many, but once you've been out on the trail awhile there is no such thing as too much food. There is nothing better than finishing a long day's hike and treating yourself to a before-dinner or after-dinner snack, especially if it contains chocolate! If I've been on the trail awhile it's not uncommon to eat one or two snacks between breakfast and lunch, another couple in the afternoon and one after my night's dinner. There are even times I might have another before I go to bed.

What are some of these snacks? Protein bars from Luna, Cliff, Harvest (Powerbar), MetRx and other protein/carb bars are a great start. Natures Valley granola bars and the Little Debbie's snacks do the job, too. Peanut butter and crackers and cheese crackers also hit the spot, and I do enjoy some Snickers bars occasionally on the trail. I didn't used to be a big chocolate fan, but on the trail it can't be beat. It's right up there with cheese.

Another good trail snack is GORP. If you are not familiar with GORP, it is traditionally known as "good ole raisins and peanuts", but that is just the starting point. I have also added M&M's, chocolate chips, huge amounts of salted mixed nuts, yogurt covered and chocolate covered raisins, cereal, cranberries, figs, dried mango, and on and on. Every mix is different, unique and delicious. I also make

GORP with dehydrated veges. Sometimes I like sweet, other times I like a crunchy salty mix.

Eating these snacks on the trail still brings me a deep sense of enjoyment and satisfaction I just don't get when I'm off the trail. I know I keep talking about comforts on the trail and GORP is definitely one of them. It's very satisfying to sit down for a break after several hard miles and enjoy a healthy snack.

Talking about food brings up another hard lesson from my earliest trip on the AT. On our first week out Paul and I shared a Lipton noodle packet and a can of tuna for dinner almost every night. You probably know where this is going, don't you? It wasn't long before we realized our error. We weren't consuming enough calories for all the hiking we were doing. Even though we were doing less than ten miles a day, our bodies had a hard time keeping up because we were burning more calories than we were taking in. After our first town resupply, we started eating our own meals and stocked up on extras like GORP and protein bars.

You Be the Judge

I like my food selection and though I have my main staples, I'm always evolving and not afraid to try new things. You can learn a great deal from other hikers when it comes to introducing new foods into your routine. Watch what others are doing and borrow some of their ideas. You can get tired of the same old foods day after day, so experiment. Just make sure you bring along a safe supply of your staple meals in case the experiment doesn't achieve the results you would like.

How Many Days of Food to Carry

How many days of food do you carry? It all depends on how many miles a day you want to hike. I usually carry a five or six-day supply, which is crazy weight wise. Six days of food can get heavy, but I do this so I won't have to visit towns more frequently than I have to. I have seen thru-hikers carry only three days of food at a time, but they do the same miles in three days that sometimes takes me five or six. It all goes back to the attitude and what kind of hike you want. Thru-hikers are out to finish the trail, not lollygag around like I did for the first two-thirds of it. They can easily put on some big miles and reap the benefits of carrying less food, therefore, less weight. I carry more in food weight so I don't have to do big days if I don't feel like it.

Planning your food is not complicated, but you better take it as serious as you do any other decision concerning your hike because you can run out. There have been a few times I've been lackadaisical in my food planning and came up short on meals. The only alternative for me was to pick up my speed and get to a town to resupply or eat the package of ramen noodles I'd been carrying around for a week! It's not fun eating ramen noodles or instant rice when you smell an assortment of tasty dinners around you. I started out liking them, but they just don't cut it after you've been on the trail for a while.

Lousy food preparation goes for other hikers, too. We have seen some crazy stuff on the trail. Once, in Georgia, we met this hiker headed to Maine. His pack looked super light and we found out why. His food rations for a day consisted of an instant shake for breakfast, a Powerbar for lunch, and macaroni and cheese for dinner. Needless to say, when we met up with him he was already eating his mac and cheese for breakfast. He could not have lasted long like that. I would guess he eventually came to his senses and acquired some real food or lost his mojo and got off the trail.

Starving yourself to save weight is not the way to hike the AT. How can anyone expect to hike several miles every day without having the fuel reserves built up from good daily nutrition? The lesson of this story is to not skimp on food to save weight. Look at everything else first, mainly your gear, then come back to the food and throw out the tuna or other heavy items you can live without.

The AT trail guides are a great reference when deciding how much food to carry. They will give you exact mileage to towns and resupply points. Below is a typical six-day supply list I use. Do yourself a favor and strip down all food of unnecessary packaging to save on weight. Ziplocs come in handy for storing and consolidating your food and serve as trash bags when you're done with your meal.

One bit of advice on cooking cleanup before we move on. There are several different ways we have seen hikers deal with their dirty dishes on the trail. I use my fingers and a bit of water to rinse out my dishes after I am done eating. This is primitive, but it works for me. Sometimes there is a bit of residue on the bottom of my pot (slightly burned food) because the heat was too high. I usually have a scrubby pad to help clean the bottom of my pot. Other hikers demand a higher degree of sanitation with their dishes and we've seen them heat up hot water and add dishwashing liquid and thoroughly clean their cooking instruments. I say do what you will, as long as you are okay with it. Contrary to warnings by others, I have never gotten sick from not washing my dishes properly.

Typical Rations for a 6-Day Hike

6 packets of instant oatmeal (two each morning for three mornings)

3 protein or breakfast bars

6 MRE entrees OR Lipton or Pasta and Cheese Dinners OR combo of each

1 package of bagels, soft-shell tortillas or loaf of bread

1 Peanut butter or a cheese block

1 cup of instant rice or soup

1 bag of dehydrated veges

2-3 packages of tuna, salmon or other meat

1 bag of GORP or beef jerky

At least 12 (15-18 is better) protein or snack Items

Instant coffee, cocoa, tea or drink mixes (and honey if you don't mind the extra weight)

Large Ziploc for trash

Olive Oil

Spices

I sometimes tote spices with me; either mixed myself in Ziploc bags or bought in a trail-sized container from Outfitters. Some of these trail spices include salt, pepper, garlic and cayenne pepper powder. I've also experimented with dehydrating my own fruits, vegetables and beef jerky months in advance while preparing for a long hike.

Ending Your Hike

It is now red flag time. If you start experiencing any of the following, you might want to consider ending your trip. It can be hard to leave the Appalachian Trail, but it is not going anywhere and will still be there when you decide to return.

Attitude Revisited

If you are not having an enjoyable hike, why are you still out there? I understand when people challenge themselves to do something. It doesn't always look pretty, but if they can accomplish their goal, it does a lot for them personally. With that aside, if someone is not enjoying the trail and isn't hell bent on finishing in one trek, why continue?

Don't let negativity ruin your trail experience. If you get to a point where you are not having fun, go home. I see hikers that get to the point of loathing the mundane; eating the same foods week in and week out, being caught in long rain spells, enduring constant blisters and aches and pains, and frankly, they look, feel and protrude unhappiness.

If you reach this point, it would be best to evaluate your situation. I'm not saying to rashly give up on the trail or yourself. Just make a decision to either see things differently and give the trail another chance or do yourself and the trail a favor and take a break or go home. I just feel the trail experience is too precious to miss out on when you are in a not-so-good frame of mind. If you experience any of these symptoms for an extended period of time, why not leave gracefully and come back another time when you are refreshed, full of energy and enthusiasm?

Physical Limitations

Another good reason to end your hike is if your body just can't take it anymore. I'm talking about something serious going on physically that might need to be checked by a professional. In your first weeks of hiking you can expect to have minor pains in different parts of your body. I would guess it is just your body getting used to the weight, impact and terrain—going beyond your normal physical activity ranges.

It is almost funny how the pain will move around to different parts of your body those first few weeks. Use caution, but don't be alarmed. You only need to worry when that pain quits moving around and stays in one spot continuously for days on end. If the same physical problem persists for days on end, it's best to assess the issue and decide if some rest is in order or a trip to an Urgent Care.

The key to avoiding injuries from the start is to allow your body time to get up to AT shape. The first few weeks are the most critical. Make sure you stretch and warm up before and after every hike. Next, take it slow. Like I mentioned earlier, do single digit days at first and take a lot of breaks. It takes me several weeks to really get trail conditioned and more to become truly and completely trail hardened – to the point where I can hike twenty plus consecutive days and it not affect me much. I know it is impossible to baby yourself for long, but you should give your body at least two weeks of low to moderate hiking before going balls to the wall. This will greatly reduce your chances of injury.

I have only encountered a few hikers with major medical problems on the trail. Our bodies are amazing machines. You can put them through the ringer and they almost always get you through. Please listen carefully to your body on the trail.

Financial Woes

By far the most disappointing reason to leave the trail has to be running out of funds. On our first AT stroll Paul and I had $700 dollars and decided to hike until we ran out of money. We budgeted well, but Father Time soon caught up with us.

It was heartbreaking for me when we had to leave the trail. We not only had gotten our trail legs by then, but were deliciously basking in the freedom. No appointments, no time cards, no alarm clocks, only the trail and walking to our next destination. Unfortunately, miles mean food, which means money!

I literally experienced the five common stages of death you learned about in Psychology class when I had to leave the AT in early July of that year. First came denial. I totally denied we would have to leave the trail even as I watched what little money we had left disappear. Next came anger. I was so upset; all I wanted to do was hike the AT and couldn't do it because of a little thing called money. Plea-bargaining came next – in a big way. Paul and I decided to take on a couple days work at a whitewater rafting company on the French Broad River in Tennessee. We moved big boulders out of a mountain stream to the edge of the river, constructing a levy. Two days later, with plenty of yellow jacket stings and no fingerprints left, we made enough dinero for a few more weeks of hiking. We picked up a few other jobs along the way, but soon realized it wouldn't be enough to sustain us through the end of the trail.

The fourth stage, depression, was all encompassing. It finally hit me that I would have to leave, like it or not. Realizing I had not fully enjoyed the past few weeks by not accepting the inevitable, I finally accepted the fact we would be leaving. Knowing my days were numbered, I once again saw the beauty of the trail and enjoyed every minute of it until we departed. I knew I would keep coming back when I could, to finish the great AT.

That was our fate by finances. Just like everything in life, you have to have the money to back up what you want to do. To help plan financially for the AT, I've always thought of it as: Prepare to spend about one dollar for every mile you hike. This is a reasonably accurate forecast for a barebones hike—one where you've already bought a lot of your food and are having it shipped. But I would suggest budgeting two dollars a mile if you plan on hiking a big portion of it. This will allow you some extra money for town visits, hostels and hotels, small gear upgrades and other associated costs.

Completion

Whether you complete the whole trail or just a section of it – congratulations! Saying you are going to hike the trail and *doing* it are two different things. I have met many people who say they want to hike the trail, but always have excuses why they can't. The only limitations we have are the ones we set ourselves. I admire people who have the desire to take on an adventure like the Appalachian Trail and go for it, and I feel sorry for all the people who grow old and never experience their dreams. I can't tell you how many people I've heard say they had wanted to hike the trail, but can't now because of X, Y and Z.

The trail is definitely a unique and life-defining experience. The experience is so complex you can't possibly know what all you've gained from it until years later. Of course the things you will notice are your strong and hardened body, new sense of confidence, inner peace, mental clarity, love and new friendships gained. There is a bond between AT hikers no matter when they hiked it. It is great to run into a fellow AT hiker here in the "real world". You can literally talk all night about your experiences.

Congratulations again for taking on the Appalachian Trail challenge. It is a huge test of the body, mind and spirit. No matter what, I hope you will have a safe, enjoyable and fulfilling experience on the legendary Appalachian Trail.

Give of Yourself

The ATC (Appalachian Trail Conservancy) and its affiliates have done a great job of keeping up the trail ascetically, functionally and politically. I urge you to either donate your time or money to maintaining the great Appalachian Trail. You will find more information on the ATC in the Appendix.

Appendix

Trial Run

The best thing you can do to get ready for the AT is to take trial runs. Go on weekend backpacking trips. Make it a mock AT trip. Take everything you would on the AT so you can have the opportunity to "shake down" your gear. Trial runs are the best tests I can recommend to prepare for the real hike. You will learn tremendous amounts of things from how to distribute the weight in your pack, how heavy a pack can really be when you actually wear it, to what kinds of foods are best for you. Paul and I did not do this and spent our first few weeks on the AT "shaking down". The fifteen pounds or so we sent home could have been eliminated if we would have taken the time to shake down at home.

Trail Magic

Trail magic is truly awesome. There is nothing like experiencing it when you are on the Appalachian Trail. Basically, trail magic can be a lot of things. You can receive food, rides, gear, money and on and on. For instance, I didn't have a sleeping mat on our very first AT hike. I was too stubborn to bring one because I wanted to save on weight. After several nights of sleeping on the hard floors of shelters, I consciously decided I would get a mat the first chance I got. Low and behold a few days later I found one on the trail! It was by a stump calling my name! Another time was when I left my camp shoes (sandals) at home. I quickly regretted it and wished I would have brought them. Well, not too much later I walked up to a shelter to camp for the night and I found a pair of extremely lightweight sandals waiting for me!

Trail magic comes in the form of food, too. One time I was hiking a particular rough and hot section of trail. It was late afternoon and I was getting low on water and conserving what I had till I got to the next spring. I came to the road to find a cooler full of Gatorades and sandwiches. What a sight to see after a long day of hot and rough hiking! There were many more instances of finding coolers on the trail; oft times with locals or ex-AT hikers manning them. They understand what it is like to hike miles upon miles every day and are true trail angels for providing nice treats for hikers. I was so inspired by all of the trail magic I received on the trail, I have done the same. I try to visit a section of trail near my home every year and set up a nice spread of food and drinks for AT hikers.

Trail magic is awesome and I could probably fill a whole book with my experiences and those I've heard about from other hikers. The next time you are on the trail and come across a cooler, open it up and realize you were too late—hikers ahead of you got all the goodies—keep the faith because there will most definitely be another opportunity at another fork in the trail before you know it.

Organizations of Interest

The Appalachian Trail Conservancy
799 Washington Street
P.O. Box 807
Harpers Ferry, WV 25425-0807
Phone: (304) 535-6331
Fax: (304) 535-2667
www.atconf.org
www.appalachiantrail.org

Leave No Trace Inc.
P.O. Box 997
Boulder, CO 80306
Phone: (303) 442-8222
Fax: (303) 442-8217
www.lnt.org

Gear Checklist

Backpack and cover
Boots or shoes and sandals
Sleeping bag
Sleeping mat
Clothes; shirts, shorts, socks and liners, fleece
   pullover
Cell Phone
Cook stove and cook set (Don't forget your
   spoon or fork)
Tent
Water filter or water treatment of some type
Trekking poles
Rain gear
Lighting
AT Literature and maps
First Aid Kit
Stuff sacks
Toiletries; hair brush, toothbrush, toothpaste, toilet
   paper, deodorant
Trowel

Optional:

Hiker pants
Bandana or hat
Reading material; book or magazine
Razor
Chapstick
Baby Wipes
Extra boot strings
Camera

CPSIA information can be obtained at www.ICGtesting.com
Printed in the USA
LVOW10s0752100716

495744LV00032B/718/P